MW01143782

Bake With Me
Chocolate Chip Cookies

Written & Illustrated
By

H.B. Scribbles

Hello my friend, how do you do?
Welcome to Bake With Me,
are you ready to make some
Chocolate Chip Cookies?

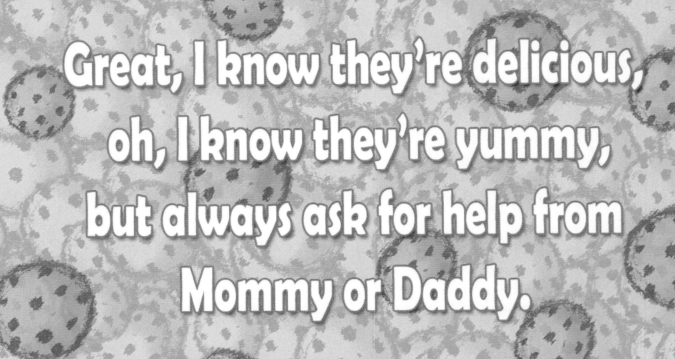

Great, I know they're delicious,
oh, I know they're yummy,
but always ask for help from
Mommy or Daddy.

There are two categories,
wet and dry,
if you look to the right you'll see
a picture of all the supplies.

1 Cup

Sugar

Flour

Chocolate Chips

Tablespoon

Egg & Yolk

Baking Soda

Brown Sugar

Salt

Teaspoon

Unsalted Butter

Measuring Cup

Vanilla Extract

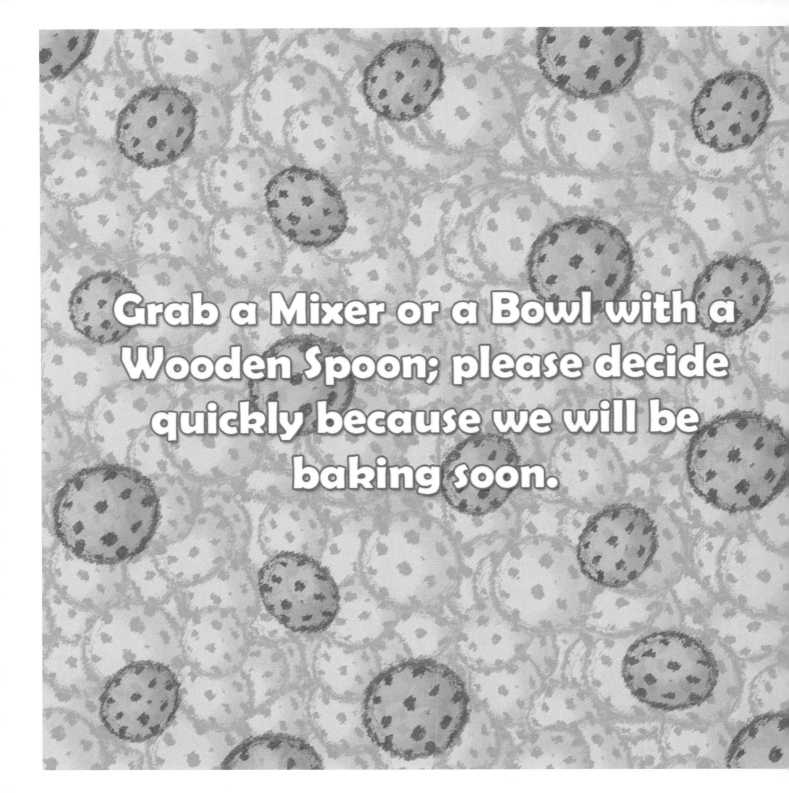

Grab a Mixer or a Bowl with a Wooden Spoon; please decide quickly because we will be baking soon.

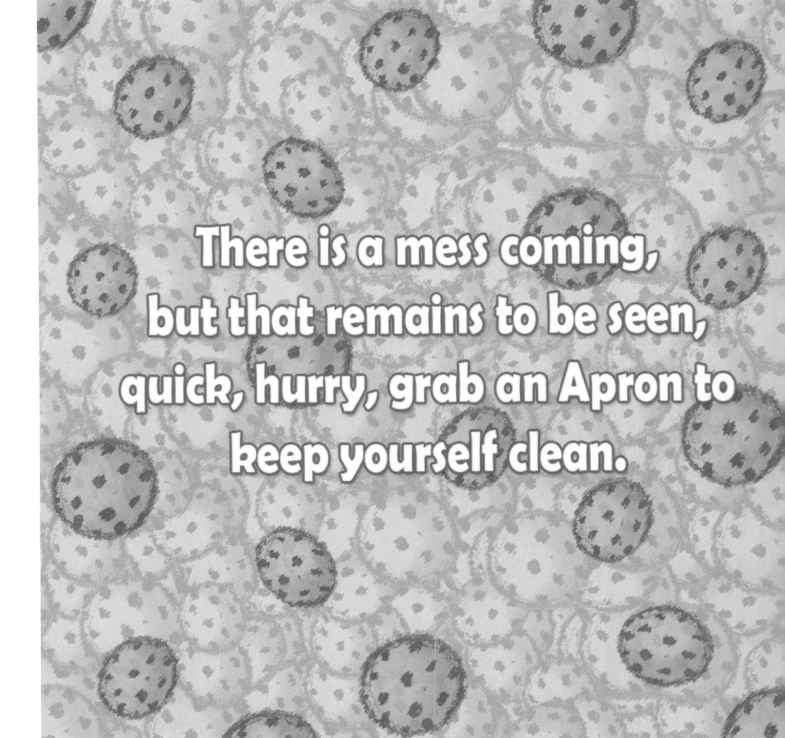

There is a mess coming,
but that remains to be seen,
quick, hurry, grab an Apron to
keep yourself clean.

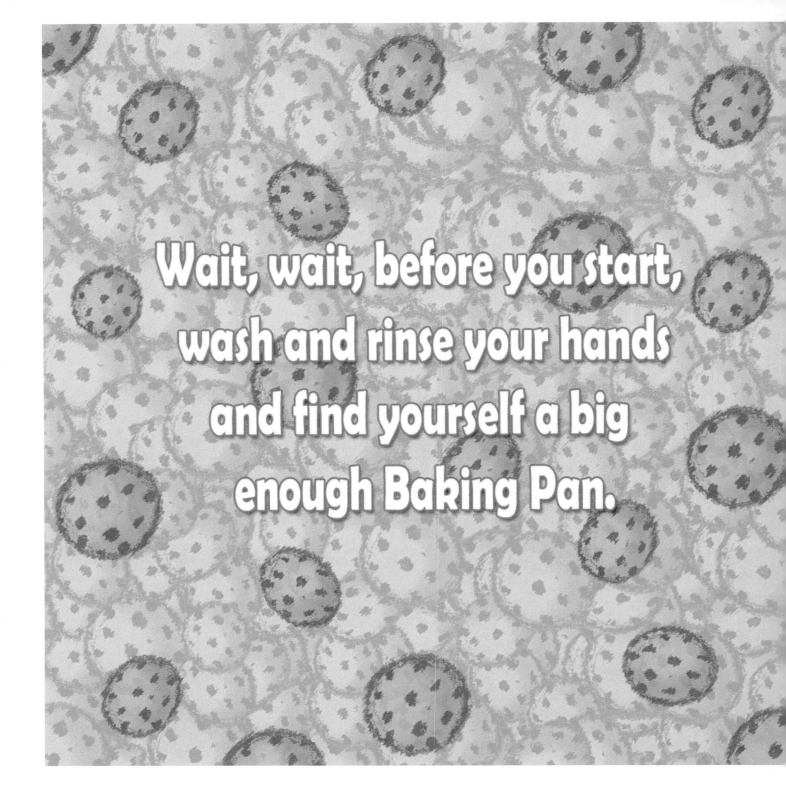

Wait, wait, before you start, wash and rinse your hands and find yourself a big enough Baking Pan.

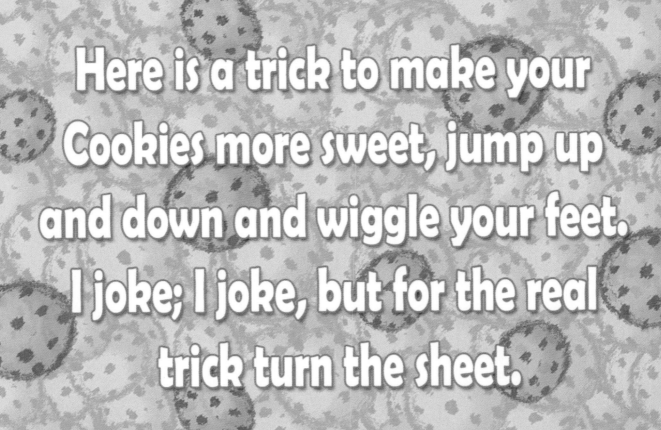

Here is a trick to make your Cookies more sweet, jump up and down and wiggle your feet. I joke; I joke, but for the real trick turn the sheet.

There is not one trick there's two,
separate the dry and wet supplies.
Mix them separately and
then together and they'll taste
better then you ever had before
I promise you.

Mix the All-Purpose Flour,
Baking Soda and a little bit of
Salt and then shake your hips.
Mix the Brown Sugar with the White,
wait and hold off on adding the
tasty Chocolate Chips.

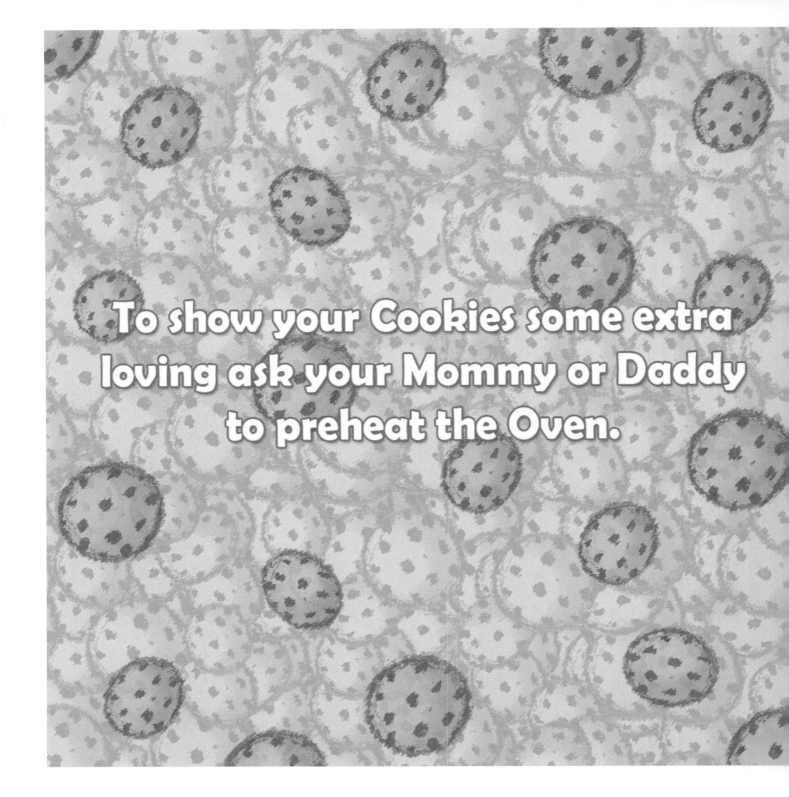

To show your Cookies some extra loving ask your Mommy or Daddy to preheat the Oven.

Now comes the best part the mixing of the Wet supplies, grab the egg and an extra yolk and mix it with the melted butter and vanilla extract, trust me Little Baker this is no joke.

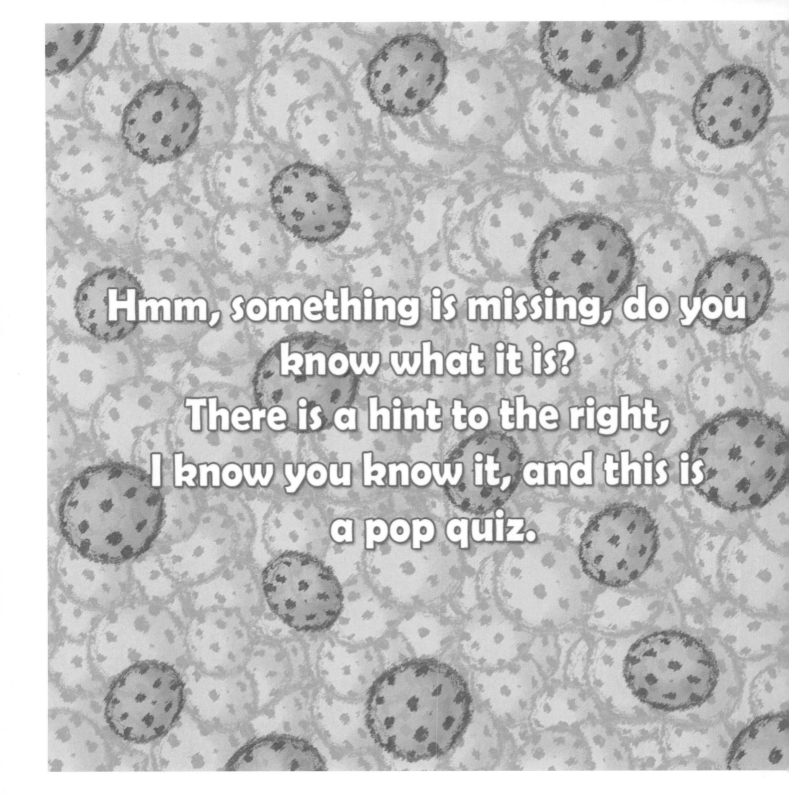

Hmm, something is missing, do you know what it is?
There is a hint to the right,
I know you know it, and this is a pop quiz.

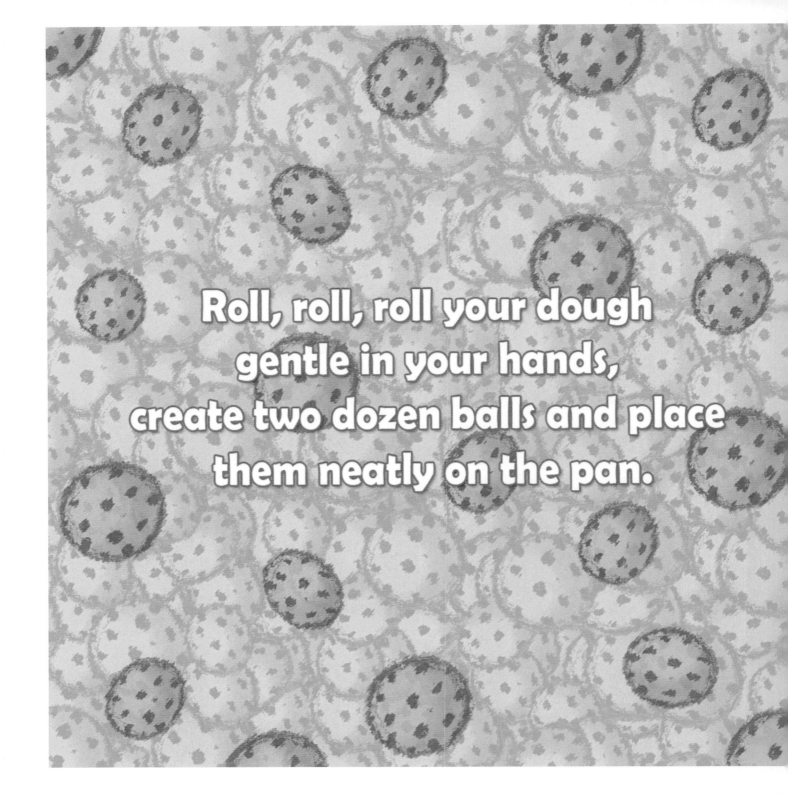

Roll, roll, roll your dough
gentle in your hands,
create two dozen balls and place
them neatly on the pan.

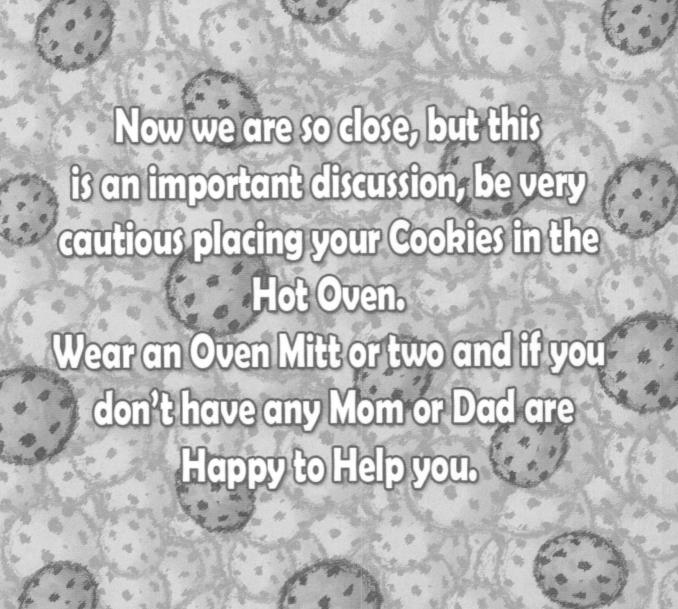

Now we are so close, but this is an important discussion, be very cautious placing your Cookies in the Hot Oven.
Wear an Oven Mitt or two and if you don't have any Mom or Dad are Happy to Help you.

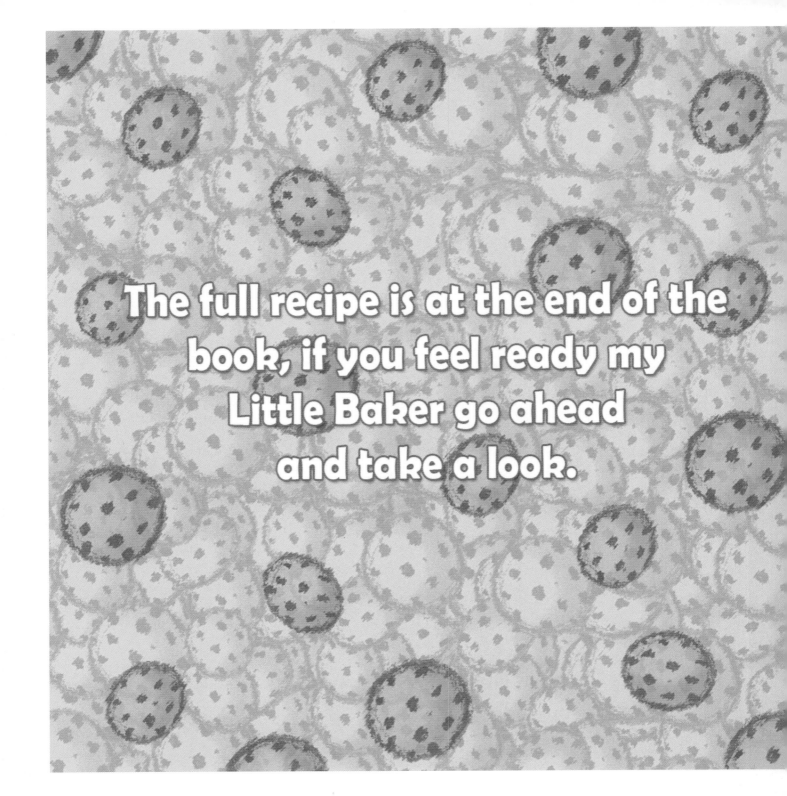

The full recipe is at the end of the book, if you feel ready my Little Baker go ahead and take a look.

Remember to Mix the dry Ingredients separate from the wet to get the best results.

Preheat the Oven to 325ºF
Bake for 15 minutes or until bottoms are golden brown.

Two Cups of All-Purpose flour
½ Teaspoon of Baking Soda
½ Teaspoon of Salt
One Cup of Brown Sugar
½ Cup of White Sugar
¾ Cup of Unsalted Butter – Melted
One Tablespoon of Vanilla Extract
One Egg Yolk
One Egg
Two Cups of Chocolate Chips

Hey Little Baker, thank you
for baking with me,
please remember to share some of
your Chocolate Chip Cookies
with your Family.